First Facts®

SCIENCE **BASICS**

WHAT IS MAGNETISM?

by Mark Weakland

raintree
a Capstone company—publishers for children
www.raintree.co.uk

Raintree is an imprint of Capstone Global Library Limited, a company incorporated in England and Wales having its registered office at 264 Banbury Road, Oxford, OX2 7DY – Registered company number: 6695582

www.raintree.co.uk
myorders@raintree.co.uk

Edited by Jaclyn Jaycox and Mari Bolte
Designed by Kyle Grentz
Original illustrations © Capstone Global Library Limited 2019
Picture research by Eric Gohl
Production by Laura Manthe
Originated by Capstone Global Library Ltd
Printed and bound in India

ISBN 978 1 4747 7086 6
23 22 21 20 19
10 9 8 7 6 5 4 3 2 1

British Library Cataloguing in Publication Data
A full catalogue record for this book is available from the British Library.

Acknowledgements
We would like to thank the following for permission to reproduce photographs: Alamy: Henry Westheim Photography, 15; Capstone Studio: Karon Dubke, 20–21; Shutterstock: Brian Goodman, 5, haryigit, 9 (top), J. Lekavicius, 17, Jakinnboaz, 11 (bottom), Nilobon Sweeney, 9 (bottom), Pixel 4 Images, 19, saicle, background (throughout), ShutterStockStudio, cover, 7, Valentyn Volkov, 11 (top), worradirek, 13.

CONTENTS

AN INVISIBLE FORCE

What can make things move but cannot be seen? It's not magic. It's **magnetism**.

Magnetism is a force. It can pull and push on objects. But the force is invisible. Let's find out more about magnetism and how it works.

magnetism natural force of a magnet, which pulls it to iron or steel

PUSH AND PULL

Magnetism comes from electrical **currents**. A current is the flow of electrical charges, such as **electrons**, through an object. The movement of these charges makes a **magnetic field**. A magnetic field around a magnet can create a force on objects in that area.

current movement of electrical charges in a
    certain direction
electron one of the tiny particles that makes up an atom
magnetic field area around a magnet or electrical current
    that can produce a force on other objects

SEEING INVISIBILITY

Iron filings make it possible to see the outline of a magnetic field. Small pieces of iron scattered around a magnet line up in the invisible field.

TYPES OF
MAGNETS

There are two basic types of magnets. A temporary magnet is made with electricity. This magnet can be turned on and off. A permanent magnet does not need electricity. Its magnetism is always working. A nail is an example of an object that can be made into a temporary magnet. A fridge magnet is a permanent magnet.

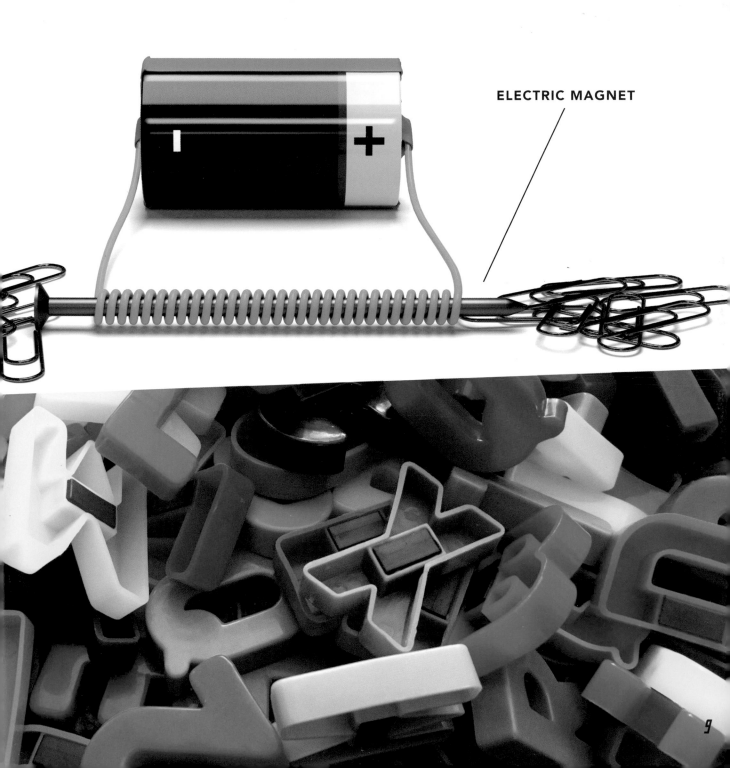

ELECTRIC MAGNET

MAGNETIC **POLES**

A magnet has two ends called *poles*. These areas have the strongest magnetic field. There is a north pole and a south pole. Opposite poles pull together. Matching poles push away from each other. For example, a north and south pole will pull together. But two south poles will always push apart.

pole one of the two ends of a magnet

NORTH AND SOUTH

More than 1,000 years ago, the first *compass* was made in China. It was a needle that acted as a magnet floating in a bowl of water. The needle always lined up in the north-south direction.

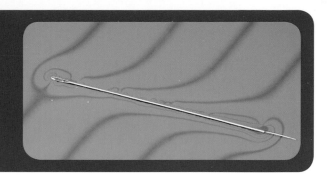

opposite poles pull together

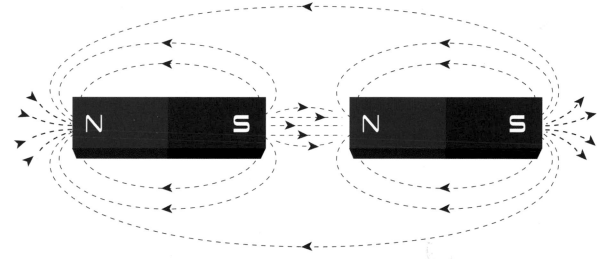

matching poles push apart

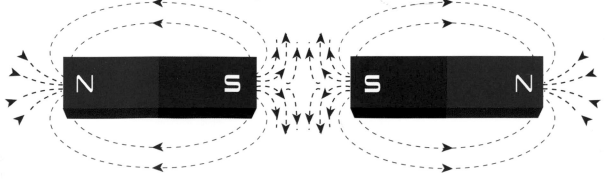

compass instrument used for finding directions

MAGNETIC
MATERIALS

Some materials are attracted to magnets. Iron, nickel, cobalt and most types of steel are common magnetic materials. This is why magnets stick to steel fridge doors. But they do not stick to wood or plastic doors.

FACT

One of the world's strongest magnets is in Florida, USA. It is stronger than 4,000 ordinary magnets. Powerful magnets such as this are used to study medicine and computers.

TRAVEL ON A
MAGLEV TRAIN

Maglev trains move very fast.
They do this by using magnets.
Two sets of magnets move the train.
One set of magnets pushes the train up.
When the train is "floating", another set
of magnets moves the train forward.

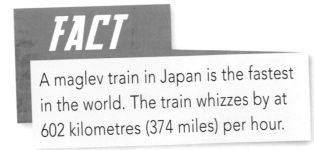

FACT

A maglev train in Japan is the fastest
in the world. The train whizzes by at
602 kilometres (374 miles) per hour.

ELECTRIC CARS

The electric motor in an electric car uses magnetism. The motor has a set of magnets. The magnets push and pull on a loop connected to a shaft. The shaft turns the wheels of the car. This *cycle* repeats again and again, making the car move forward.

cycle set of events that happen over and over again

17

MAKING
NOISE

Speakers use magnets to make sounds. Each speaker has two magnets. The first one uses electricity. The second one does not. The first magnet gets stronger when a lot of electricity flows through it. These magnets work together to make a cone in the speaker move back and forth. The movement creates sound waves that we can hear.

CAN YOU HEAR ME?

Speakers can be found in many places and in many things. Sound systems have big speakers. Mobile phones have tiny ones. Stadiums and cinemas have speakers. Where else can speakers be found?

19

MAGNETISM **EXPERIMENT**

WHAT DOES A MAGNET ATTRACT?

MATERIALS:

- bowl of small objects such as safety pins, marbles, erasers, paper clips, sweets and keys
- string
- large magnet

WHAT TO DO:

1. Make a list of the objects in the bowl.

2. Make a prediction about what will happen when you lower the magnet into the bowl. What objects will cling to the magnet? What objects will not? Write, draw or say your prediction.

3. Tie a string around the magnet. Then lower the magnet into the bowl and move it around. Observe what happens. What objects cling to the magnet?

4. Check your prediction. How does what you observed compare to your prediction?

GLOSSARY

compass instrument for finding directions

current movement of electrical charges in a certain direction

cycle set of events that happen over and over again

electron one of the tiny particles that make up an atom

magnetism natural force of a magnet that pulls it to iron or steel

magnetic field area around a magnet or electrical current that can produce a force on other objects

pole one of the two ends of a magnet